Holiday Cooking for Kids

by Janet Wilk

Ideals Publishing Corp.
Milwaukee, Wisconsin

CONTENTS

ISBN 0-8249-3014-2
Copyright © MCMLXXXII by Janet Wilk
All rights reserved.
Printed and bound in the United States of America.

Published by Ideals Publishing Corporation
11315 Watertown Plank Road
Milwaukee, Wisconsin 53226
Published simultaneously in Canada

about this book . . .

Cooking can be fun. This cookbook will help you dazzle your parents as well as your friends with all the good recipes it contains. There are recipes for special occasions, holidays, snacks, after-school treats and gifts for relatives and friends. All of the recipes are rated according to the following key:

A   advanced
B   intermediate
C   easy

Be sure to check with an older person to find out when is a convenient time for you to make a recipe. Read the recipe all the way through before you start to cook. Assemble all of the necessary equipment and ingredients before you start to cook. If you measure all of the ingredients and place them on a tray before you begin to cook, you won't leave out an ingredient.

An important part of cooking is cleaning up when you are finished. The best cooks clean up as they go along. As you finish using a utensil, *except sharp knives,* put it in warm, soapy water to soak. Then clean up will go faster when you have finished cooking. Always wash sharp knives separately *or* get an adult to do this. Rinse utensils that have held egg, milk or mashed potatoes in cold water before placing them in warm, soapy water. Wash, dry and put away all utensils after cooking. Wash the counters and leave the kitchen neat and clean.

Be sure to read the next few pages before you start cooking. They will explain some basic cooking terms and techniques that you should know.

Also, be sure to enjoy what you have cooked and take pride in sharing it.

INTRODUCTION

HOW TO MEASURE

Successful cooking adventures depend on correct measuring. It pays to be accurate. Always use special measuring cups and spoons, not the kind you use when you eat.

HOW TO MEASURE DRY INGREDIENTS

Flour & sugar	Spoon from canister into dry measuring cup. Level with metal spatula or straight side of table knife.
Powdered sugar	Same as for flour and sugar. If powdered sugar is lumpy, sift it before measuring.
Brown sugar	Spoon into dry measure, packing it down firmly with back of spoon. Level with metal spatula or straight side of table knife.
Baking mix	Spoon lightly into dry measuring cup set on wax paper. Level with metal spatula or straight side of table knife. Baking mix will be lumpy. Pour excess on paper back into box.
Baking powder, baking soda, cornstarch, cream of tartar, salt and spices	Dip and fill measuring spoon to overflowing. Level with metal spatula or straight side of table knife. Don't pack down.

HOW TO MEASURE LIQUID INGREDIENTS

A glass measuring cup has a 1 or 2-cup mark below the rim so you won't spill. The cup also has a lip to make pouring easy. Place the cup on the counter to measure. Bend down so that you can see exactly when you have filled the cup to the correct measure.

HOW TO MEASURE BUTTER, MARGARINE & SHORTENING

1. Butter and margarine are sold in wrappers that are marked off in tablespoons, ¼-cup and ½-cup amounts. Cut butter or margarine with sharp knife following line on paper. If it is not marked, measure as you would measure solid shortening.

2. To measure solid shortening, pick cup or spoon that holds amount desired. Pack shortening so there won't be any air left in cup or spoon. Level off top with metal spatula or straight edge of table knife.

3. Measure liquid shortening as you would other liquids.

HOW TO PEEL & CHOP

Cut away from yourself when you use a vegetable peeler or a sharp knife. Hold the vegetable in one hand, the peeler in the other. Watch out for your fingers. Check with an older person before you use a sharp knife. Ask him or her to show you which knife to use. If you are slicing, dicing or chopping, do not hold the food in your hand. Use a wooden cutting board, *not* the countertops. Watch an older person use a sharp knife to slice, dice or chop before you try it.

COOKING SAFELY

1. Always wash your hands before you start to cook. Dry them thoroughly to avoid slippery fingers. Always wear an apron. If you have long hair, tie it back away from your face.

2. Before you use a sharp knife, can opener, broiler, blender or electric mixer, be sure an older person is in the kitchen to help you.

3. Be careful when you drain foods cooked in hot water. Be sure to wear oven mitts or use pot holders and slightly turn your face away from the steam so it won't burn you. Start by draining small amounts of food. Call an older person to drain large amounts of food like macaroni or spaghetti.

INTRODUCTION

4. Wipe up spills immediately to avoid slippery floors.

5. Always turn the sharp edge of a knife or vegetable peeler away from you and your hand when you chop, slice or peel foods.

6. Always use thick dry pot holders, not thin wet ones, and you won't burn yourself. Use pot holders to steady the handle of a saucepan while you stir, to take hot dishes and pans and baking sheets out of the oven and to pull out or push in hot oven racks. Set hot pans and baking sheets on a wire rack to cool.

7. Turn off the blender and hand-held or counter mixer before you scrape the sides of the container or bowl so the rubber scraper won't get caught in the blades.

8. Be sure to turn off and unplug the hand-held or counter mixer before removing the beaters.

9. Never disconnect an appliance by pulling the cord. Pull the plug instead.

10. Be sure to turn off the oven or range after you finish cooking. When the range has cooled, wipe it clean with a wet sponge or dish cloth.

11. Stir a hot mixture on the range with a wooden spoon or a metal spoon with a wooden or heavy plastic handle. An all-metal spoon will get hot enough to burn your hand.

12. Keep dish towels and pot holders away from the burners on the range and the heating coils in the oven of an electric stove, and away from the flame of a gas stove.

13. Put foods into boiling water gently so the water won't splash and burn you.

14. Always lift lids on hot pots with the opening away from you so the steam won't burn you.

15. Do not put hot grease into water or water into hot grease or it will sputter.

16. Do not use water to put out a grease fire. Water only makes it worse. To put out a grease fire, turn off the oven or burner, stand back and toss handfuls of dry baking soda at the base of the flame. Call for help.

OVEN RULES

1. Arrange shelves before you turn on the oven.

2. Allow plenty of space around each dish you are baking, being sure no containers touch.

3. Alternate foods on each shelf so that one is not directly over another.

4. Use tight-fitting covers or aluminum foil when a recipe calls for covering a pan during cooking.

5. Open the oven door carefully. Always use pot holders or oven mitts when inserting or removing dishes.

6. Close the oven door quickly so heat will not be lost.

RANGE RULES

1. Put large pans on large burners; small pans on small burners.

2. Turn pan handles so they don't stick out over the edge of the range where they can easily be bumped or tipped over.

3. Make sure pan handles are not over another burner, especially if that burner is on.

COOKING TERMS

Bake	To cook in the oven.
Baste	To pour or brush liquid over food while it cooks.
Batter	A thick, beaten mixture of liquid and dry ingredients to be cooked or baked.
Beat	To make mixture smooth by mixing fast with beater or spoon.
Blend	To mix ingredients until smooth and uniform. To whirl in an electric blender.
Boil	To cook until liquid is bubbling and steaming.
Bring to a boil	To cook over high heat until liquid bubbles.
Broil	To cook directly over coals or under heat of broiler.
Brown	To cook on each side until a food changes color, usually in a small amount of fat over medium heat.
Chill	To place in the refrigerator to lower the temperature.
Chop	To cut in pieces with a knife on a cutting board.
Coat	To roll or stir food in nuts, shredded coconut, bread crumbs, etc., until all sides are evenly covered.
Combine	To mix ingredients.

Cool	Allow to return to room temperature.
Core	Cut out the stem end and remove the seeds.
Cream	To beat until smooth, soft and fluffy.
Crumble	To break into small pieces with your hands.
Cube	To cut food into pieces with 6 sides that are usually larger than ¼ inch.
Cut in	To mix shortening with dry ingredients using a pastry blender or 2 table knives.
Dash	Less than ⅛ teaspoon of an ingredient; a few grains or drops.
Dice	To cut food into small cubes of same size and shape.
Dot	To put small pieces of one food on top of another, such as butter over pie filling.
Dough	A thick, sticky mixture of flour or meal, liquids and various dry ingredients, baked as bread or pastry.
Drain	Pour off liquid or let it run off through the holes in a sieve or colander.
Flour	To coat with flour.
Fold	To mix ingredients gently with a rubber spatula, whisk or spoon. Cut down through mixture, go across bottom of bowl, then up and over, close to surface of mixture.
Fry	To cook in hot fat.
Garnish	To decorate finished dish with colorful food to make it look pretty.
Grate	To rub food on a food grater that breaks it up into very fine particles.
Grease	To rub pan surface with fat to prevent sticking.
Knead	To fold, turn and press dough with heel of hand.
Ladle	To dip and serve liquid with a ladle.

Melt	To make liquid by heating.
Mince	To cut or finely chop food into tiny pieces.
Mix	To stir foods together.
Pare	To cut off the skin.
Peel	To remove outer skin.
Pinch	The amount of dry ingredient you can hold between your thumb and first finger.
Pit	To take out the seeds.
Preheat	To heat oven to a certain temperature before putting food in to cook.
Refrigerate	Place in the refrigerator.
Scald	To heat milk just below boiling point. You'll see tiny bubbles around the edge.
Sift	To put dry ingredients (flour) through sifter or sieve.
Simmer	To cook in liquid over low heat so bubbles form slowly.
Slice	To cut food crosswise into pieces.
Soften	To let ingredients sit at room temperature until they are soft enough to spread.
Sprinkle	To scatter in small drops or tiny pieces.
Stir	To mix around and around with a spoon or fork. Usually, you stir with a spoon, but use a fork to stir pastry.
Thaw	To set frozen food at room temperature until it is no longer frozen.
Toss	To mix foods lightly.
Well	A hole made in dry ingredients in which you pour liquid.
Whip	To beat rapidly. Use rotary beater to whip cream or to beat egg whites until light and fluffy. Beating adds air.

NEW YEAR'S CELEBRATION

New Year's Day is not always celebrated by watching parades and football games on television. In fact, the holiday hasn't always been celebrated on Jan. 1! Hundreds of years ago, the new year was a time to welcome the harvest season. Children received money and clothing gifts. This year, start the New Year with a simple meal or snack that you prepare all by yourself!

CHOCO-MELBA   A

MAKES: 6 servings
PREPARATION TIME: 10 minutes
INGREDIENTS:
    Hot chocolate mix
    Whipped cream or topping
¼ cup raspberry syrup
EQUIPMENT:
 6 mugs

1. Make 6 mugs of hot chocolate according to package directions.
2. Place heaping spoonful of whipped cream in each mug.
3. Drizzle with raspberry syrup.

CHEESE TWISTS   A

MAKES: 6 to 8 servings
PREPARATION TIME: 45 minutes; 12 minutes to bake
INGREDIENTS:
 1 17¼-ounce package frozen puff pastry sheets
 ½ cup butter or margarine
 ½ cup grated Parmesan cheese
 2 tablespoons poppy seeds
EQUIPMENT:
    small saucepan
    pastry brush
    10 × 15-inch baking sheet
    table knife
    metal spatula
    wire rack

1. Thaw puff pastry sheets in package for 30 minutes.
2. Preheat oven to 425°.
3. Melt butter in saucepan over low heat.
4. Place pastry sheets on counter.
5. Brush with melted butter, using pastry brush.
6. Sprinkle with cheese and poppy seeds.
7. Cut each lengthwise into 2 rectangles, using table knife.
8. Cut each rectangle crosswise into ½-inch strips.
9. Twist strips and place on baking sheet. Bake 10 to 12 minutes.
10. Use spatula to remove twists from baking sheet. Place on wire rack to cool.

NEW YEAR'S CELEBRATION

CHINESE NEW YEAR CRUNCH A

MAKES: 4 servings
PREPARATION TIME: 20 minutes; 10 minutes to bake

INGREDIENTS:
½ cup butter *or* margarine
1 tablespoon soy sauce
¼ teaspoon garlic salt
¼ teaspoon onion salt
1 5-ounce can chow mein noodles *or* 5 ounces pretzel sticks
1 cup square rice cereal
1 cup peanuts

EQUIPMENT:
small saucepan
10 × 15-inch jelly roll pan
wooden spoon

1. Preheat oven to 275°.
2. Melt butter in saucepan.
3. Add soy sauce, garlic and onion salts and stir with wooden spoon.
4. Spread chow mein noodles, rice cereal and peanuts on jelly roll pan.
5. Drizzle with butter mixture and stir to coat.
6. Bake 5 minutes; stir well and bake another 5 minutes until light brown.
7. Cool and store in airtight container.

ORANGE BLOSSOM CHICKEN WINGS B

MAKES: 6 servings
PREPARATION TIME: 10 minutes; 45 minutes to bake

INGREDIENTS:
3 pounds chicken wings, tips removed, *or* 3 pounds chicken pieces
½ cup catsup
2 tablespoons orange marmalade
2 tablespoons light brown sugar, packed
2 tablespoons vinegar
1 tablespoon prepared mustard
1 teaspoon garlic salt

EQUIPMENT:
9 × 13-inch baking pan
small mixing bowl
mixing spoon

1. Preheat oven to 350°.
2. Arrange wings in 1 layer in pan.
3. Mix remaining ingredients in bowl with spoon. Pour over chicken.
4. Bake 45 minutes.
Note: Recipe can be prepared in advance through step 3 and refrigerated *or* frozen. Chicken also can be cooked over a charcoal fire.

CARNIVAL VEGETABLE BOWL B

MAKES: 6 to 8 servings
PREPARATION TIME: 25 minutes; 2 hours to chill

INGREDIENTS:
1 small head cauliflower
2 cups cherry tomatoes
2 small zucchini
1 cup vegetable oil
½ cup vinegar
1 ¾-ounce package Italian dressing mix

EQUIPMENT:
table knife
large mixing bowl
mixing spoon
plastic wrap

1. Cut cauliflower into bite-size pieces using table knife. Place in bowl.
2. Add tomatoes.
3. Cut zucchini into thin slices with table knife and add to bowl.
4. Pour oil, vinegar and dressing mix over vegetables.
5. Stir well, using mixing spoon.
6. Cover with plastic wrap and chill 2 hours.
7. Uncover and drain before serving.
Note: Bottled Italian dressing can be substituted for oil, vinegar and dressing mix.

RICE AND NOODLE BAKE   B

MAKES: 6 servings
PREPARATION TIME: 10 minutes; 2 hours
   to bake

INGREDIENTS:
   ¾ cup uncooked brown rice
   1 2-ounce envelope dry chicken
      noodle soup mix
   2 cups water
   1 tablespoon butter
EQUIPMENT:
      1-quart casserole with lid *or*
      aluminum foil
      mixing spoon

   1. Preheat oven to 300°.
   2. Mix all ingredients in casserole with
spoon.
   3. Cover with lid *or* foil.
   4. Bake 2 hours.
   5. Toss rice to separate pieces.
   Note: White rice can be substituted for
brown rice. Cooking time will be 1 hour 15
minutes.

CHOCOLATE ECLAIR PUDDING C

MAKES: 8 servings
PREPARATION TIME: 20 minutes; 1 hour
   to chill

INGREDIENTS:
   1 4-ounce package instant vanilla
      pudding mix
   1 10-ounce frozen pound cake,
      thawed
   ½ cup chocolate syrup
   1 cup whipped cream *or* whipped
      topping
      Maraschino cherries to garnish,
      optional
EQUIPMENT:
      mixing bowl
      table knife
      1½-quart glass serving bowl
      spoon
      plastic wrap

   1. Prepare pudding in mixing bowl
according to package instructions.
   2. Cut cake into 1-inch cubes, using
table knife.
   3. Place ⅓ of cake cubes in bottom of
glass bowl.
   4. Pour ⅓ of syrup over cubes.
   5. Pour some pudding over cake and
drizzle with more chocolate syrup.
   6. Repeat layers in this order until all
ingredients are used.
   7. Spoon whipped cream on top.
   8. Cover with plastic wrap and chill until
serving time. Decorate with maraschino
cherries just before serving, if desired.
   Note: This can be made 1 day in advance. Ladyfingers could be substituted for
pound cake.

VALENTINE'S DAY

Even your great great grandmother probably waited for a lace and paper love note on this holiday. Valentine's Day has been celebrated for hundreds of years every February 14. Surprise the family and prepare a special dinner. Make some pretty treats for your school friends to say Happy Valentine's Day!

BERRY GOODY   C

MAKES: 6 servings
PREPARATION TIME: 10 minutes

INGREDIENTS:

  1 banana
  ¼ cup frozen orange juice concentrate, thawed
  1 10-ounce package frozen strawberries, partially thawed
  1 cup plain yogurt
  2 cups cranberry juice cocktail

EQUIPMENT:

  blender
  rubber spatula

  1. Peel banana and place in blender with juice concentrate and strawberries.

  2. Blend at high speed 10 seconds. Use spatula to scrape down sides of blender container.

  3. Add yogurt and juice. Blend until smooth.

  4. Pour into 6 glasses.

Note: Frozen raspberries could be substituted for strawberries. Also, fresh strawberries could be used, but be sure to add 2 tablespoons granulated sugar.

PARTY PIZZA BITES   B

MAKES: about 50 pizzas
PREPARATION TIME: 30 minutes; 20 minutes to bake

INGREDIENTS:

  2 cups buttermilk biscuit mix
  1 10-ounce bulk sausage meat, uncooked
  1 8-ounce package (2 cups) shredded mozzarella cheese
  ¼ cup tomato sauce
  1 teaspoon oregano

EQUIPMENT:

  medium-size mixing bowl
  dry measuring cups
  liquid measuring cup
  measuring spoons
  mixing spoon
  pastry blender
  cookie sheet

  1. Preheat oven to 350°.

  2. Measure biscuit mix into mixing bowl. Add all other ingredients.

  3. Mix the biscuit mix into the other ingredients with the pastry blender until well blended. Use your hands, if you must.

  4. Shape mixture with teaspoon into balls about the size of walnuts. Place on ungreased cookie sheet, about 1 inch apart.

  5. Place in oven; bake for about 20 minutes. Serve hot.

Note: Pizzas can be refrigerated or frozen after step 3.

VALENTINE'S DAY

LITTLE CHEF'S SOUP FOR TWO   B

MAKES: 2 servings
PREPARATION TIME: 45 minutes

INGREDIENTS:
  1 carrot
  2 cherry tomatoes
  1 strip green pepper
  1 10-ounce can chicken broth
  ¼ cup very thin egg noodles
    dash salt and pepper
EQUIPMENT:
    sharp knife
    chopping board
  1 quart saucepan
    wooden spoon

1. Peel carrot and chop into small pieces with knife on chopping board.
2. Cut each tomato in half.
3. Cut green pepper into small pieces.
4. Combine ingredients in saucepan. Stir.
5. Place over low heat; cook for 30 minutes. Serve hot.

HAWAIIAN FISH KEBABS   B

MAKES: 4 servings
PREPARATION TIME: 20 minutes; 20 minutes to bake

INGREDIENTS:
  1 green pepper
  1 9-ounce package fish sticks, partially thawed
  1 8-ounce can pineapple chunks, drained
  ¼ cup maraschino cherries
  ½ cup sweet and sour sauce
EQUIPMENT:
    table knife
  4 8-inch metal skewers
    pastry brush
    wire rack
    shallow baking pan

1. Preheat oven to 450°.
2. Cut green pepper into 1-inch squares, using table knife.
3. Cut each fish stick into thirds.
4. Alternate pieces of green pepper, fish, pineapple chunks and maraschino cherries on skewers.
5. Brush each kebab with some sweet and sour sauce, using pastry brush.
6. Place rack in pan.
7. Place kebabs on rack. Bake 15 to 20 minutes *or* until fish is light brown.

CARA'S VALENTINE   A

MAKES: 6 servings
PREPARATION TIME: 25 minutes; 3 to 4 hours to freeze

INGREDIENTS:
  15 marshmallows *or* 1½ cups miniature marshmallows
  1 tablespoon milk
  1 cup dairy sour cream
  1 10-ounce box frozen strawberries *or* raspberries
    Curly lettuce leaves to garnish
EQUIPMENT:
    wooden spoon
  1 ½-quart saucepan
  5 to 6 cup heart-shaped pan *or* 9 × 5-inch loaf pan
    plastic wrap

1. Use wooden spoon to stir marshmallows and milk in saucepan over *very* low heat until marshmallows melt. Remove from heat.
2. Stir in sour cream.
3. Stir in strawberries until separated and distributed throughout cream.
4. Pour into mold. Cover with plastic wrap.
5. Freeze 3 to 4 hours.
6. Unmold onto platter about 20 minutes before serving. Garnish with lettuce leaves around side of mold.

SWEETHEART KISS B

MAKES: 24 pieces
PREPARATION TIME: 25 minutes; 5 minutes to bake

INGREDIENTS:
  1 cup peanut butter
  1 cup granulated sugar
  1 egg
  ½ teaspoon vanilla
    Chocolate candy kisses, unwrapped

EQUIPMENT:
  10 × 15-inch baking sheet
  small mixing bowl
  mixing spoon
  teaspoon
  metal spatula

1. Preheat oven to 350°. Grease baking sheet.

2. Mix peanut butter, granulated sugar, egg, and vanilla in bowl using mixing spoon.

3. Shape dough into 1-inch balls, using teaspoon to help.

4. Place about 2 inches apart on baking sheet.

5. Bake 5 minutes. Do *not* overbake.

6. Immediately place chocolate candy kiss in center of each.

8. Cool on baking sheet before removing, using spatula. Store in airtight tin.

PINK LADY'S VALENTINE CAKE B

MAKES: 12 servings
PREPARATION TIME: 35 minutes; 25 minutes to bake

INGREDIENTS:
  1 18-ounce package white *or* yellow cake mix
  1 3-ounce package strawberry-flavored gelatin
  ½ cup vegetable oil
  ½ cup frozen strawberries with juice, thawed
  ¼ cup water
  ½ cup dairy sour cream
  4 eggs
  4 cups sweetened whipped cream *or* whipped topping
  6 to 12 marshmallows
    Pink sugar crystals

EQUIPMENT:
  1 9-inch round cake pan
  1 9-inch square cake pan
  large mixing bowl
  mixing spoon
  wire racks
  table knife
  kitchen scissors

1. Preheat oven to 350°. Grease pans.

2. Put cake mix, gelatin, oil, strawberries, water, sour cream and eggs in mixing bowl.

3. Stir with mixing spoon until well mixed.

4. Divide batter evenly between pans.

5. Bake 25 minutes *or* until center of cake springs back when touched with mitt-covered finger.

6. Cool in pans on racks.

7. When cool, remove cake layers from pans.

8. Cut round cake in half, using table knife.

9. Place square cake on large serving platter.

10. Place round halves on 2 sides of square cake to form heart-shaped cake.

11. Frost with whipped cream.

12. Snip marshmallows with scissors into thirds to form "petals."

13. Dip cut edge of "petals" into sugar crystals to color center.

14. Arrange marshmallow "petals" to form several flowers on top of cake.

15. Chill until serving time.

ST. PATRICK'S DAY

We must all have a bit of the Irish in us because we all enjoy "the wearing of the green" and the fun of St. Patrick's Day. St. Patrick, the patron saint of Ireland, gave us the shamrock, a popular good luck sign. Treat your family to a supper fit for a leprechaun.

BIT-O-BLARNEY BURGERS   A

MAKES: 6 servings
PREPARATION TIME: 15 minutes; 10 minutes to cook

INGREDIENTS:
- 1 baking potato
- 1 pound ground beef
- 1 tablespoon instant minced onion
- 1 tablespoon catsup
- 1 teaspoon salt
-    dash ground black pepper
- 6 hamburger buns

EQUIPMENT:
- vegetable peeler
- vegetable grater
- mixing bowl
- 10-inch skillet
- metal spatula

1. Peel potato with vegetable peeler and shred into mixing bowl.
2. Mix in ground beef, onion, catsup, salt and pepper.
3. Shape mixture into 6 patties.
4. Heat skillet over medium heat 1 minute.
5. Arrange patties in skillet. Cook 5 minutes on each side. Use spatula to turn burgers and to remove from skillet.
6. Serve on buns.

SPICY SHAMROCK BISCUITS   A

MAKES: 10
PREPARATION TIME: 10 minutes; 8 minutes to bake

INGREDIENTS:
- 1 10-ounce package refrigerator buttermilk biscuits
- 2 tablespoons butter or margarine
- 1 tablespoon Italian seasoning

EQUIPMENT:
- 10 × 15-inch baking sheet
- kitchen scissors
- small saucepan
- pastry brush
- metal spatula

1. Preheat oven to 375°.
2. Place biscuits about 2 inches apart on baking sheet.
3. Snip each with scissors to resemble shamrock.
4. Spread slightly so biscuits take shape of shamrock.
5. Melt butter in saucepan over low heat.
6. Brush each biscuit "shamrock" with butter using pastry brush.
7. Sprinkle some seasoning over each biscuit.
8. Bake 8 minutes. Use spatula to remove from baking sheet.

Bit-O-Blarney Burgers, this page; Potaddies, page 16; Cream Cheese Shamrocks, page 16; St. Pat's Parfaits, page 17

ST. PATRICK'S DAY

POTADDIES   A

MAKES: 6 servings
PREPARATION TIME: 20 minutes; 30 minutes to bake

INGREDIENTS:
- 4 baking potatoes
- 2 tablespoons vegetable oil
- ¼ cup butter or margarine, softened
  Salt and ground black pepper

EQUIPMENT:
- sharp knife
- 10 × 15-inch baking pan
- table knife
- metal spatula

1. Preheat oven to 400°.
2. Cut potatoes lengthwise in ½-inch slices using sharp knife.
3. Drizzle oil over bottom of pan.
4. Spread 1 teaspoon of butter with table knife on side of each potato slice as if buttering bread.
5. Place potato slices, buttered-side-up, in pan.
6. Bake 25 to 30 minutes or until light brown and slightly crisp.
7. Sprinkle with salt and pepper. Remove from pan using spatula. Serve immediately.

CREAM CHEESE SHAMROCKS   A

MAKES: 6 servings
PREPARATION TIME: 25 minutes

INGREDIENTS:
- 6 lettuce leaves
- 1 large green pepper
- 2 stalks celery
- 6 radishes
- 2 3-ounce packages cream cheese with chives, softened
  Finely chopped parsley or chives to garnish

EQUIPMENT:
- 6 salad plates
- sharp knife
- small mixing bowl
- mixing spoon

1. Place lettuce leaf on each of 6 salad plates.
2. Slice off stem end of pepper with sharp knife. Cut into 6 ¼-inch rings. Remove seeds.
3. Place ring on lettuce.
4. Chop celery and radishes into small pieces.
5. Mix cream cheese, celery and radishes in mixing bowl using mixing spoon.
6. Divide mixture among rings, mounding cheese in center.
7. Sprinkle with parsley or chives, if desired.

LEPRECHAUNS   B

MAKES: 24
PREPARATION TIME: 20 minutes; 10 minutes to bake

INGREDIENTS:
- ½ cup solid vegetable shortening
- 1 cup granulated sugar
- 1 egg
- ¼ cup molasses
- 2 cups flour
- 1 teaspoon each: ground ginger, ground cloves, and ground cinnamon
- 1 tablespoon baking soda
  Raisins

EQUIPMENT:
- large mixing bowl
- mixing spoon
- 10 × 15-inch baking sheet
- wire rack
- metal spatula

1. Preheat oven to 350°.

2. Mix shortening, sugar, egg and molasses in mixing bowl using mixing spoon.

3. Stir in flour, spices and baking soda.

4. Shape dough into 24 walnut-size balls.

5. Place 2 inches apart on baking sheet.

6. Place raisins on each to make eyes, nose and mouth.

7. Bake 8 to 10 minutes.

8. Cool on racks. Use spatula to remove from baking sheet. Store in airtight tin.

KORIN'S KOOKIES   B

MAKES: 48

PREPARATION TIME: 30 minutes; 40 minutes to bake 4 sheets of cookies

INGREDIENTS:
- 1 cup light brown sugar, packed
- 1 cup butter *or* margarine, softened
- 2 cups quick-cooking rolled oats
- 1 cup flour
- 1 teaspoon baking soda
- Granulated sugar

EQUIPMENT:
- mixing bowl
- baking sheet
- glass
- metal spatula

1. Preheat oven to 350°.

2. Place all ingredients except granulated sugar in mixing bowl.

3. Mix *with your hands*, squeezing and mashing until well mixed.

4. Form dough into 48 balls.

5. Place about 2 inches apart on baking sheet.

6. Grease bottom of glass and dip into granulated sugar. Use glass to flatten dough balls.
Dip in additional sugar when necessary.

7. Bake 10 minutes.

8. Cool slightly. Remove from baking sheet using spatula. Store in airtight tin.

ST. PAT'S PARFAITS   C

MAKES: 6 servings

PREPARATION TIME: 20 minutes plus chilling time

INGREDIENTS:
- 25 to 30 chocolate wafers
- 1 cup sweetened condensed milk
- 1 6-ounce can frozen limeade, thawed
- 1 8-ounce container whipped topping *or* 1 cup whipped cream
- Green food coloring
- 2 tablespoons chocolate jimmies

EQUIPMENT:
- blender
- mixing bowl
- mixing spoon
- 6 parfait glasses *or* bowls

1. Put wafers in blender. Process until crumbs form.

2. Pour milk and limeade into mixing bowl. Stir well with mixing spoon.

3. Stir in topping.

4. Add 1 or 2 drops food coloring and gently mix.

5. Place 2 or 3 spoonfuls of mixture in each parfait glass. Sprinkle with 1 tablespoon crumbs. Continue layering cream and crumbs, ending with cream.

6. Sprinkle 1 teaspoon jimmies on top of each parfait. Refrigerate until serving time.

EASTER

Are chocolate bunnies and candy eggs part of your Easter morning? Every child's family has its own special way to celebrate this spring holiday. Treat your family to a tasty breakfast "pizza" or to delicious creamy cupcakes!

SUNRISE PIZZA   A

MAKES: 4 servings
PREPARATION TIME: 30 minutes; 5 minutes to bake

INGREDIENTS:
  4 English muffins, split, toasted and buttered
  8 thin slices dried chipped beef
  4 eggs
  1 teaspoon instant minced onion
  2 tablespoons milk
  ½ teaspoon salt
     Dash ground black pepper
  2 tablespoons butter or margarine
  8 slices American cheese

EQUIPMENT:
     10 × 15-inch baking sheet
     small bowl
     rotary beater or wire whisk
     9 or 10-inch skillet
     metal spatula

1. Preheat oven to 400°.
2. Place muffins on baking sheet.
3. Top each with 1 slice beef.
4. Beat eggs in small bowl using rotary beater. Add minced onion, milk, salt and pepper.
5. Melt butter in skillet over medium heat. Heat until bubbling.
6. Add egg mixture. Stir occasionally with spatula until eggs are set, but still soft. Remove from heat.

7. Spoon eggs onto muffins.
8. Top each with a cheese slice.
9. Bake 5 minutes or until cheese melts and bubbles. Remove from baking sheet with spatula and serve immediately.

GREEK EASTER BASKET ROLLS   B

MAKES: 8
PREPARATION TIME: 2 hours; 20 minutes to bake

INGREDIENTS:
  1 1¾-ounce package hot roll mix
  8 eggs

EQUIPMENT:
     2-quart mixing bowl
     mixing spoon
     10 × 15-inch baking sheet
     tea towel
     wire rack
     metal spatula

1. Prepare mix according to package illustrations using mixing bowl and spoon.
2. Cover dough and let rise until double in bulk.
3. Grease baking sheet.
4. Uncover dough and punch down with your fist.
5. Divide dough into 8 portions.
6. Remove small piece of dough from each portion. Form remaining dough into hamburger-pattie shape. Repeat with remaining portions.
7. Place 8 large patties 3 to 4 inches apart on baking sheet.
8. Carefully press egg in its shell into center of each patty.
9. Form remaining 8 pieces of dough into pencil shapes.
10. Arrange over egg in decorative manner.

24 Karat Cupcakes, page 20; Candy Easter Eggs, page 21

11. Cover with towel, put in warm place and let rise 30 minutes.

12. Bake 20 minutes or until bread is brown. Remove from baking sheet with spatula and place on rack to cool.

Note: Eggs in their shells cook as the bread bakes.

PASTEL EASTER EGG   C

MAKES: 12 servings
PREPARATION TIME: 30 minutes; 3 hours
   to freeze
INGREDIENTS:
  1 pint *each:* lemon, lime, orange and
     raspberry sherbet, softened
 ¾ cup fudge sauce
  1 ¾-ounce tube decorating gel
     Easter candies to garnish
EQUIPMENT:
    2-quart egg-shaped mold *or* 2-quart
    round bottom mixing bowl
    ice cream scoop
    tablespoon
    plastic wrap
    tea towel
    serving platter

1. Spoon 1 pint of sherbet into mold using ice cream scoop.

2. Smooth with back of tablespoon.

3. Layer remaining sherbet into mold.

4. Cover with plastic wrap.

5. Freeze 2 to 3 hours.

6. Soak towel in very warm water and then wring out when ready to serve.

7. Place towel over inverted mold on serving platter.

8. When mold is loose, remove it.

9. Pour sauce over egg.

10. Write Happy Easter over top with gel.

11. Surround egg with Easter candies and serve immediately.

24 KARAT CUPCAKES   B

MAKES: 30 1¾-inch cupcakes
PREPARATION TIME: 30 minutes; 15 minutes to bake
INGREDIENTS:
  2 eggs
 ¾ cup vegetable oil
 ½ cup granulated sugar
  1 cup flour
  1 teaspoon baking powder
 ½ teaspoon salt
  1 teaspoon ground cinnamon
  1 cup grated carrot
 ½ cup chopped nuts
  1 cup prepared white frosting
 ½ cup orange-tinted coconut
     Rabbit-shaped Easter candies,
     optional
EQUIPMENT:
 24 1¾-inch cupcake tins *or* 12 2¾-inch
     cupcake tins
     mixing bowl
     mixing spoon
     wire rack

1. Preheat oven to 350°. Grease tins.

2. Mix eggs, oil, sugar, flour, baking powder, salt, cinnamon, carrot and nuts in mixing bowl using mixing spoon.

3. Fill cupcake tins ⅔ full.

4. Bake 15 minutes for 1¾-inch tins; 20 minutes for 2¾-inch tins.

5. Cool on rack.

6. Remove from tins and frost each cupcake. Sprinkle each with tinted coconut.

7. Place "bunny" in middle of each cupcake, if desired.

Note: To tint coconut, place 1 teaspoon water in small mixing bowl. Add few drops orange food coloring and stir until coconut is evenly colored.

COCONUT NEST CAKE   B

MAKES: 12 servings
PREPARATION TIME: 30 minutes; 55 minutes to bake

INGREDIENTS:

1 18-ounce package yellow cake mix
1 3¾-ounce package coconut cream instant pudding mix
1 cup flaked coconut
3 eggs
1½ cups water
¼ cup vegetable oil
1 16½-ounce can white frosting
2 cups flaked coconut
   Jelly beans
   Chocolate eggs *or* other Easter candies

EQUIPMENT:

   10-inch tube pan
   mixing bowl
   mixing spoon
   wire rack
   table knife

1. Preheat oven to 350°. Grease pan.
2. Beat cake mix, pudding mix, coconut, eggs, water and oil in mixing bowl with mixing spoon until smooth.
3. Pour in pan.
4. Bake 50 to 55 minutes.
5. Cool on rack 15 minutes.
6. Turn cake out onto rack and cool completely.
7. Frost with white frosting using table knife.
8. Cover with coconut, lightly pressing into frosting.
9. Place jelly beans, chocolate eggs *or* other Easter candies around cake.
Note: Cake can be baked in layer pans or 9 by 12-inch pan according to package directions.

CANDY EASTER EGGS   C

MAKES: 24 eggs
PREPARATION TIME: 20 minutes; 40 minutes to chill

INGREDIENTS:

1 3-ounce package cream cheese, softened
2½ cups powdered sugar
½ teaspoon vanilla *or* almond *or* lemon *or* raspberry *or* coconut extract
   Food coloring, optional
   Assorted pastel-colored sugar crystals

EQUIPMENT:

   mixing bowl
   mixing spoon
   teaspoon
   wax paper
   10 × 15-inch baking sheet

1. Mix cream cheese, powdered sugar and extract in bowl with mixing spoon.
2. Stir in 1 or 2 drops of food coloring, if desired. Chill 30 minutes.
3. Form rounded teaspoons of mixture into egg shapes.
4. Roll in colored sugar.
5. Cover baking sheet with wax paper.
6. Place sugar-coated eggs on sheet.
7. Chill until set, 30 to 40 minutes. Store in refrigerator.

MOTHER'S DAY/ FATHER'S DAY

Both Mother's Day and Father's Day are "new" holidays which began in this century. Mother's Day, observed the second Sunday in May, is a celebration of love between mother and child. Many children love to surprise Mom with breakfast in bed. Then they may treat her to cards, flowers and sweets.

Father's Day occurs soon after Mother's Day. Dad's special day is celebrated on the third Sunday in June. Many children like to honor their father with a meal prepared just for him!

BEST-EVER SAUSAGES   A

MAKES: 4 servings
PREPARATION TIME: 20 minutes
INGREDIENTS:
  2 tablespoons butter *or* margarine
  1 10-ounce package precooked breakfast sausage links
  ¼ cup light brown sugar, packed
  2 tablespoons soy sauce
  2 tablespoons frozen apple juice concentrate, thawed
EQUIPMENT:
  large skillet

1. Melt butter in skillet. Add sausages and cook, turning occasionally until evenly browned.

2. Add remaining ingredients and cook over medium heat until the mixture bubbles. Serve immediately.

HEARTY BREAKFAST OMELET   A

MAKES: 4 servings
PREPARATION TIME: 15 minutes

INGREDIENTS:
  6 eggs
  ¾ cup milk
  ¾ teaspoon salt
    Dash ground black pepper
  1 cup bread crumbs
  3 tablespoons butter *or* margarine
EQUIPMENT:
  1 mixing bowl
  rotary beater *or* wire whisk
  10-inch skillet
  metal spatula

1. Beat eggs, milk, salt and pepper in bowl, using rotary beater.

2. Stir in bread crumbs.

3. Heat butter in skillet until it sizzles.

4. Add eggs. Cook until brown on 1 side.

5. Turn with spatula. Cook other side. Serve immediately.

Hearty Breakfast Omelet, this page; Best-Ever Sausages, this page; French Bran Puffs, page 24; Morning Glory, page 24

MOTHER'S DAY/FATHER'S DAY

FRENCH BRAN PUFFS   B

MAKES: 1 dozen
PREPARATION TIME: 25 minutes; 20 minutes to bake

INGREDIENTS:
- 2 eggs
- 2 tablespoons honey
- ¼ cup vegetable oil
- ½ cup milk
- 1 cup bran-flake cereal
- 2 cups flour
- 2 teaspoons baking powder
- ¼ teaspoon salt
- 2½ teaspoons ground cinnamon
- ¼ cup raisins, optional
- ½ cup granulated sugar

EQUIPMENT:
- 1 12-cup cupcake tin
- 2 small mixing bowls
  rotary beater *or* wire whisk
  medium-size mixing bowl
  mixing spoon
  table knife

1. Preheat oven to 375°. Grease tin.
2. Beat eggs, honey, oil and milk in small mixing bowl with rotary beater. Stir in cereal with mixing spoon.
3. Mix flour, baking powder, salt, ½ teaspoon cinnamon and raisins in medium-size mixing bowl.
4. Stir egg mixture gently into dry ingredients. Do not overmix.
5. Fill tins ⅔ full with batter.
6. Bake 20 minutes.
7. Combine sugar and 2 teaspoons cinnamon in small mixing bowl.
8. Remove warm muffins from tin with table knife.
9. Roll each in cinnamon-sugar mixture. Serve warm.

MORNING GLORY   B

MAKES: 4 servings
PREPARATION TIME: 10 minutes

INGREDIENTS:
- 1 6-ounce can frozen orange juice concentrate, thawed
- 1 egg
- 1 tablespoon honey
- 1 cup plain yogurt
- 1 cup milk

EQUIPMENT:
- blender
- 4 tall glasses

1. Put all ingredients in blender.
2. Blend until frothy.
3. Pour in glasses. Serve immediately.

HOT CHICKEN SALAD   B

MAKES: 4 to 6 servings
PREPARATION TIME: 25 minutes; 40 minutes to bake

INGREDIENTS:
- 3 cups cooked chicken or turkey chunks
- 2 hard-cooked, diced eggs, optional
- 1 10½-ounce can cream of chicken soup
- 1 teaspoon instant minced onion
- ¾ cup mayonnaise
- 1 tablespoon lemon juice
- 2 large stalks celery
- 2 strips green pepper
- 1 tablespoon butter *or* margarine
- 15 potato chips

EQUIPMENT:
- large mixing bowl
  kitchen scissors
  mixing spoon
- 1 ½-quart casserole
  plastic bag
  rolling pin

1. Preheat oven to 350°.
2. Put chicken, eggs, soup, onion, mayonnaise and lemon juice in bowl.

3. Cut celery and pepper into small pieces with scissors. Add to bowl.

4. Stir with mixing spoon.

5. Grease casserole with butter. Pour chicken mixture into casserole.

6. Crush potato chips in plastic bag by rolling with rolling pin.

7. Sprinkle over chicken mixture.

8. Bake 30 to 40 minutes. Serve immediately.

DAD'S FAVORITE HERO   A

MAKES: 4 servings

PREPARATION TIME: 20 minutes; 30 minutes to cook

INGREDIENTS:

1 cup barbecue sauce
2 cups chili sauce
1 pound lean ground beef
1 egg
1 tablespoon instant minced onion
2 tablespoons catsup
½ cup quick-cooking rolled oats
½ teaspoon garlic salt
4 hero rolls, split

EQUIPMENT:

large skillet
mixing bowl
mixing spoon
fork
wooden spoon

1. Mix barbecue sauce and chili sauce in skillet.

2. Heat on low.

3. Stir ground beef, egg, onion, catsup, oats and garlic salt in mixing bowl using mixing spoon.

4. Shape into small meatballs.

5. Arrange meatballs in hot sauce. Cook 15 minutes over low heat without stirring.

6. Turn meatballs carefully using fork. Cook 15 minutes.

7. Divide meatballs among rolls. Spoon some sauce over meatballs using wooden spoon. Serve immediately.

PEANUT BUTTER CUP SQUARES   A

MAKES: 2 pounds

PREPARATION TIME: 20 minutes

INGREDIENTS:

1 cup butter *or* margarine
1½ cups graham cracker crumbs
1 teaspoon vanilla
1 cup peanut butter
2½ cups powdered sugar
1 12-ounce package semisweet chocolate chips

EQUIPMENT:

2 quart saucepan
dry measuring cups
measuring spoons
9 × 13 × 2-inch metal baking pan
wooden spoon
small saucepan
straight-edged spatula
table knife

1. Melt butter in saucepan over low heat.

2. Remove from heat.

3. Stir in graham cracker crumbs.

4. Add vanilla, peanut butter and powdered sugar. Mix well.

5. Spread peanut butter mixture evenly in baking pan with spoon.

6. Pour chocolate chips into small saucepan. Cook over low heat until melted. Watch carefully so chocolate does not burn.

7. Carefully spread melted chocolate with spatula over peanut butter mixture.

8. Place in refrigerator until firm, about 30 minutes.

9. Remove from refrigerator; let stand for 15 minutes to soften chocolate slightly.

10. Cut into small squares with table knife.

11. Each square can be separately wrapped in plastic wrap for gift giving.

4TH OF JULY/ SUMMER FUN

Fireworks, parades and picnics lead off a summer of fun for young and old alike. The 4th of July, Independence Day, is the day to be proud of the great red, white and blue of our flag. Let the 4th be the beginning of many summer treats that you make.

FIRECRACKERS   C

MAKES: 4 to 6 servings
PREPARATION TIME: 10 minutes
INGREDIENTS:
  1 6-ounce can frozen grape juice concentrate, thawed
  4 cups prepared lemon-lime carbonated beverage
  1 pint vanilla ice cream
EQUIPMENT:
  3-quart pitcher
  mixing spoon
  4 to 6 glasses
  ice cream scoop

1. Pour concentrate into pitcher.
2. Stir in beverage using mixing spoon.
3. Put 2 scoops ice cream into each glass using ice cream scoop.
4. Pour grape drink over ice cream.
5. Serve immediately with straw, if desired.

TACO DIP   A

MAKES: 4 servings
PREPARATION TIME: 30 minutes

INGREDIENTS:
  ½ pound ground beef
  1 teaspoon instant minced onion
  4 tablespoons taco seasoning mix *or* 2 tablespoons chili powder
  ½ cup catsup *or* tomato sauce
  1 8-ounce can *or* 1 cup refried beans
  1 large tomato
  1 cup shredded Cheddar cheese
     Large-size corn chips *or* tortilla chips
EQUIPMENT:
  9-inch skillet
  wooden spoon
  sharp knife
  8-inch pie pan *or* round shallow pan

1. Cook ground beef in skillet until light brown.
2. Stir in onion, seasoning mix, catsup and refried beans with wooden spoon. Cook over low heat 10 to 15 minutes.
3. Chop tomato into small pieces using sharp knife.
4. Pour beef mixture in center of pan.
5. Make ring of chopped tomato around meat.
6. Make ring of cheese around tomatoes.
7. Serve hot as spread with corn chips.

Chick & Chips, page 28; Summer Day Salad, page 28; Layered Tomato Salad, page 29; Firecrackers, this page

4TH OF JULY/SUMMER FUN

TUNA TACO POCKETS   A

MAKES: 4 servings
PREPARATION TIME: 20 minutes

INGREDIENTS:
- 1 7-ounce can tuna, drained
- ½ cup dairy sour cream
- 1 tablespoon taco seasoning mix
- 2 large lettuce leaves
- 1 tomato
- ½ cup shredded Monterey Jack *or* Cheddar cheese
- 2 large Syrian *or* pocket breads

EQUIPMENT:
- fork
- small mixing bowl
- mixing spoon
- sharp knife

1. Chop tuna with fork in mixing bowl. Stir in sour cream and seasoning mix with mixing spoon.
2. Shred lettuce with knife. Chop tomatoes into bite-size pieces.
3. Cut each piece of bread in half, resulting in 4 pockets.
4. Put ¼ of lettuce in each pocket.
5. Scoop ¼ of tuna mixture over lettuce.
6. Sprinkle ¼ of cheese into each pocket. Top with tomatoes. Serve immediately.

SEA DOGS   B

MAKES: 8 sandwiches
PREPARATION TIME: 15 minutes; 20 minutes to bake

INGREDIENTS:
- 8 slices bacon
- 1 8-ounce package frozen fish sticks
- 8 hot-dog buns
- Tartar Sauce

EQUIPMENT:
- broiling pan with rack
- kitchen tongs

1. Preheat oven to 425°.
2. Wrap 1 piece of bacon around each fish stick.

3. Place on rack in pan.
4. Bake 20 minutes or until bacon is slightly crisp.
5. Put "sea dog" in bun using tongs.
6. Spoon some tartar sauce over each "sea dog." Serve immediately.

CHICK & CHIPS   B

MAKES: 6 servings
PREPARATION TIME: 15 minutes; 50 minutes to bake

INGREDIENTS:
- ½ cup evaporated milk
- ½ teaspoon poultry seasoning
- 3 cups finely crushed potato chips
- 10 to 12 chicken legs

EQUIPMENT:
- 8 × 10-inch baking dish
- 2 deep plates *or* shallow bowls

1. Preheat oven to 375°. Generously grease dish.
2. Mix evaporated milk and poultry seasoning in deep plate.
3. Spread crushed chips on another deep plate.
4. Dip each chicken piece first in milk mixture and then in chips.
5. Place in baking dish.
6. Bake 40 to 50 minutes *or* until meat is tender.

SUMMER DAY SALAD   A

MAKES: 6 servings
PREPARATION TIME: 15 minutes; overnight to chill

INGREDIENTS:
- 1 8-ounce can green beans, drained
- 1 8-ounce can sliced carrots, drained
- 1 8-ounce can sliced potatoes, drained
- 1 large tomato
- 1 cup Italian salad dressing
- 1 tablespoon instant minced onion
- ¼ teaspoon garlic powder
- ½ cup mayonnaise

EQUIPMENT:
    mixing bowl
    mixing spoon
    sharp knife
    plastic wrap

1. Combine vegetables in mixing bowl using mixing spoon.

2. Take core out of tomato and chop into small pieces using sharp knife.

3. Add to bowl with dressing, onion and garlic powder. Stir.

4. Cover with plastic wrap. Refrigerate overnight.

5. Drain dressing from vegetables when ready to serve.

6. Stir in mayonnaise. Serve immediately.

Note: Green peppers make handy serving "bowls." Cut off stem end and scoop out seeds and any white membrane. Spoon salad into peppers. Place on serving platter and surround with lettuce to garnish.

BANANA WALDORF SALAD   C

MAKES: 4 servings
PREPARATION TIME: 20 minutes; 30 minutes to chill

INGREDIENTS:
    1 8-ounce can pineapple chunks, drained
    1 large stalk celery
    ½ cup walnut pieces
    ¼ cup maraschino cherries
    ½ cup whipped cream *or* whipped topping
    ½ cup mayonnaise
    2 teaspoons lemon juice
    2 bananas
    4 lettuce leaves
       Maraschino cherries to garnish
EQUIPMENT:
    medium-size mixing bowl
    kitchen scissors
    mixing spoon

    table knife
    4 salad plates

1. Put pineapple in mixing bowl.

2. Cut celery into small pieces with kitchen scissors. Add to pineapple in bowl.

3. Stir in walnuts, cherries, whipped cream, mayonnaise and lemon juice.

4. Peel bananas. Cut into crosswise slices using table knife and add to bowl. Stir gently to combine.

5. Chill 30 minutes.

6. Place 1 lettuce leaf on each of 4 plates when ready to serve. Divide salad among plates. Garnish with piece of maraschino cherry. Serve immediately.

LAYERED TOMATO SALAD   A

MAKES: 4 to 6 servings
PREPARATION TIME: 25 minutes; 3 hours to chill

INGREDIENTS:
    4 large tomatoes
    1 cup fresh parsley
       Fresh basil, chopped, *or* dried basil
    ¾ cup Italian salad dressing
EQUIPMENT:
    sharp knife
    kitchen scissors
    1-quart serving bowl
    plastic wrap

1. Cut core out of tomatoes and slice thinly using knife.

2. Snip parsley into small pieces using scissors.

3. Place 1 layer of tomatoes in bottom of bowl. Sprinkle with some basil and parsley.

4. Continue layering tomatoes, basil and parsley.

6. Pour dressing over top.

7. Cover with plastic wrap. Chill 2 to 3 hours before serving.

10-LAYER SALAD

MAKES: 6 to 8 servings

PREPARATION TIME: 30 minutes plus chilling time

INGREDIENTS:

1 cup mayonnaise
¼ cup dairy sour cream
1 teaspoon instant minced onion
½ teaspoon salt
1 head lettuce, washed
1 10-ounce package frozen baby peas, thawed
1 2-ounce bottle green olives
1 8-ounce package mozzarella or Cheddar cheese, shredded

EQUIPMENT:

small mixing bowl
mixing spoon
2-quart salad bowl
kitchen scissors
plastic wrap

1. Mix mayonnaise, sour cream, onion and salt in mixing bowl using mixing spoon. Set aside.

2. Tear lettuce into bite-size pieces using fingers.

3. Spread ½ lettuce in salad bowl. Top with ½ peas.

4. Cut olives into small pieces with scissors. Spread ½ over peas.

5. Spoon ½ of mayonnaise mixture over olives. Sprinkle ½ of cheese over mayonnaise.

6. Repeat layers 1 more time, beginning with lettuce and ending with cheese.

7. Cover with plastic wrap. Refrigerate until serving time.

VEGETABLE GARDEN PARMESAN   A

MAKES: 4 servings

PREPARATION TIME: 20 minutes; 30 minutes to bake

INGREDIENTS:

1 small zucchini
1 small green pepper
1 large tomato
1 small onion, peeled
¼ teaspoon dried basil
¼ teaspoon salt
¼ teaspoon garlic salt
Dash ground black pepper
2 tablespoons butter
4 ounces mozzarella cheese slices
¼ cup grated Parmesan cheese

EQUIPMENT:

1 ½-quart casserole
sharp knife
foil

1. Preheat oven to 375°. Grease casserole.

2. Cut zucchini into thin slices using sharp knife. Spread on bottom of casserole.

3. Cut pepper into thin strips and spread on top of zucchini.

4. Slice tomato and spread over peppers.

5. Slice onion thinly and spread over tomatoes.

6. Sprinkle basil, salt, garlic salt and pepper over top.

7. Cut butter into small pieces and evenly distribute over top.

8. Cover with cheese slices. Sprinkle with Parmesan cheese.

9. Cover with foil.

10. Bake 30 minutes.

11. Remove foil carefully; bake 10 minutes *or* until cheese is light brown. Serve immediately.

Yankee Doodle Dandy Pie, page 32

4TH OF JULY/SUMMER FUN

BANANA SPLIT PIE   C

MAKES: 8 servings
PREPARATION TIME: 20 minutes; 2 hours
  to chill

INGREDIENTS:
- 1 quart vanilla ice cream, softened
- 1 9-inch graham cracker piecrust
- 2 bananas
- 1 8-ounce can crushed pineapple, well drained
- 1 cup frozen strawberries, thawed and well drained
- 1½ cups whipped cream *or* topping
- ½ cup chocolate syrup

EQUIPMENT:
  ice cream scoop
  table knife
  spoon

1. Scoop ice cream into crust using ice cream scoop.

2. Peel bananas and cut into ¼-inch slices using table knife. Spread evenly over ice cream.

3. Spoon pineapple and then strawberries over bananas.

4. Cover with whipped cream.

5. Freeze 1 or 2 hours.

6. Cut into 8 pieces and drizzle with chocolate syrup when ready to serve. Serve immediately. Store leftovers in freezer.

SODA-POP POPSICLES   C

MAKES: about 12
PREPARATION TIME: 10 minutes plus time
  to freeze

INGREDIENTS:
- 4 cups orange soda
- 1 14-ounce can sweetened condensed milk
- 1 cup pineapple juice

EQUIPMENT:
  mixing spoon
  popsicle molds with wooden popsicle sticks
  foil

1. Stir all ingredients in mixing bowl with mixing spoon.

2. Pour into popsicle molds. Cover with foil. Insert wooden popsicle sticks through foil. Freeze until firm.

YANKEE DOODLE DANDY PIE   A

MAKES: 6 to 8 servings
PREPARATION TIME: 30 minutes; 3 hours
  to chill

INGREDIENTS:
- 1 3¼-ounce package vanilla pudding mix
- 1 8-ounce package cream cheese, softened
- ½ teaspoon vanilla
- 1 8-inch graham cracker piecrust
- 20 to 25 strawberries, hulled
- 1 pint blueberries
- Whipped cream *or* topping, optional

EQUIPMENT:
  medium-size saucepan
  rotary beater
  mixing spoon

1. Prepare pudding mix in saucepan according to package directions.

2. Remove from heat and add cream cheese. Beat with rotary beater until smooth.

3. Stir in vanilla using mixing spoon.

4. Pour into crust.

5. Refrigerate 3 hours *or* overnight.

6. Place strawberries in circle around outer edge of pie and put 1 large strawberry in center of pie just before serving. Place blueberries to fill in remaining area.

7. Serve with whipped cream, if desired.

4TH OF JULY/SUMMER FUN

STRAWBERRY CHEESECAKE BARS   B

MAKES: 24
PREPARATION TIME: 30 minutes; 30 minutes to bake

INGREDIENTS:
- 2 tablespoons butter *or* margarine, softened
- 1 18-ounce package oatmeal cookie mix
- 1 cup strawberry jam
- 1 8-ounce package cream cheese, softened
- ¼ cup granulated sugar
- 2 eggs
- 1 teaspoon vanilla

EQUIPMENT:
- 2 mixing bowls
- pastry blender
- rubber spatula *or* table knife
- rotary mixer
- 9 × 13-inch baking pan
- metal spatula

1. Preheat oven to 350°.
2. Cut butter into cookie mix in bowl using pastry blender. Set aside ½ cup crumbs for topping.
3. Press remaining mixture into bottom of pan.
4. Spread jam evenly over mixture with spatula.
5. Beat cream cheese until smooth in mixing bowl with rotary mixer. Add sugar, eggs and vanilla. Beat until smooth.
6. Pour over jam. Sprinkle evenly with reserved ½ cup cookie mixture.
7. Bake 30 minutes.
8. Cool slightly in pan. Cut into 24 bars. Use spatula to remove from pan. Store in airtight tin.

OLD GLORIES   B

MAKES: 24
PREPARATION TIME: 20 minutes; 10 minutes to bake

INGREDIENTS:
- ½ cup butter *or* margarine
- 1 cup light brown sugar, packed
- 1 egg
- 1 teaspoon vanilla
- 2 tablespoons milk
- 1 cup flour
- ½ teaspoon salt
- ¼ teaspoon baking powder
- ½ teaspoon baking soda
- ½ cup raisins

EQUIPMENT:
- 10 × 15-inch baking sheet
- 2-quart mixing bowl
- mixing spoon
- teaspoon
- metal spatula
- wire rack

1. Preheat oven to 325°. Grease baking sheet.
2. Stir butter, brown sugar, egg, vanilla and milk in mixing bowl with mixing spoon until smooth.
3. Stir in flour, salt, baking powder and baking soda.
4. Stir in raisins.
5. Drop 3 inches apart by rounded teaspoonfuls onto baking sheet.
6. Bake 6 to 8 minutes *or* until brown.
7. Remove from baking sheet with spatula and cool on wire rack. Store in airtight tin.

HALLOWEEN TREATS

A witch? A ghost? A goblin? Which will you be this All Hallows Eve? Along with tricks, be sure to have some homemade treats on hand for every witch and scarecrow that comes your way!

WITCHES' BREW CIDER   A

MAKES: 4 servings
PREPARATION TIME: 15 minutes
INGREDIENTS:
- 2 cups apple cider
- 1 6-ounce can frozen lemonade concentrate, thawed
- 1 cup water
- 4 cinnamon sticks
  Lemon slices, optional

EQUIPMENT:
- 2-quart saucepan
- mixing spoon
- 4 cups *or* mugs

1. Pour cider, concentrate and water into saucepan. Stir with mixing spoon.

2. Warm over medium heat.

3. Pour into cups. Put 1 cinnamon stick in each. Serve immediately.

SKILLET SOMBRERO PIE   A

MAKES: 6 servings
PREPARATION TIME: 45 minutes
INGREDIENTS:
- 1 pound ground beef
- 1 10-ounce package frozen corn, thawed
- 1 8-ounce can tomato sauce
- 1 16-ounce can tomatoes
- 1 tablespoon instant minced onion
- 1 1¾-ounce package chili seasoning mix
- 1 6-ounce package corn chips
- ½ cup grated Cheddar cheese

EQUIPMENT:
- wooden spoon
- large deep skillet

1. Stir ground beef with wooden spoon in skillet over medium heat until beef browns.

2. Stir in corn, tomato sauce, tomatoes, onion and seasoning mix.

3. Turn heat to low. Simmer 20 minutes.

4. Arrange chips in ring around edge of skillet.

5. Sprinkle cheese in center and cook until cheese melts, 3 to 5 minutes.

6. Serve pie directly from skillet.

Skillet Sombrero Pie, this page; Witches' Brew Cider, this page; Monster Cookies, page 37

HALLOWEEN TREATS

HALLOWEEN SALAD   A

MAKES: 6 servings

PREPARATION TIME: 20 minutes plus chilling time

INGREDIENTS:
- 1 3-ounce package orange-flavored gelatin
- 1 cup boiling water
- 1 16-ounce can mandarin oranges, undrained
- 1 8-ounce can crushed pineapple, drained
- 1 pint orange sherbet
  Mayonnaise

EQUIPMENT:
- mixing bowl
- mixing spoon
- 6-cup mold *or* round bowl
- serving platter *or* plate

1. Put gelatin in mixing bowl.
2. Stir in water with mixing spoon until gelatin dissolves.
3. Stir in oranges, pineapple and orange sherbet.
4. Pour into mold.
5. Freeze until firm.
6. Unmold on platter and use spoonfuls of mayonnaise to make jack-o'-lantern face on top of gelatin salad.

DEVIL'S DARK CHOCOLATE PUDDING   B

MAKES: 6 to 8 servings

PREPARATION TIME: 25 minutes; 35 minutes to bake

INGREDIENTS:
- 2 eggs
- ¾ cup dairy sour cream
- ¼ cup vegetable oil
- 1 18-ounce package chocolate cake mix
- 1 7½-ounce package chocolate frosting mix
- ¼ cup margarine

EQUIPMENT:
- 9-inch square cake pan
- mixing spoon
- medium-size mixing bowl
- table knife

1. Preheat oven to 350°.
2. Lightly grease bottom and sides of pan.
3. Beat eggs with mixing spoon in mixing bowl. Add sour cream and oil.
4. Stir in dry cake mix until batter is smooth.
5. Spread ½ batter in pan.
6. Sprinkle with ½ dry frosting mix.
7. Repeat with remaining batter and frosting mix.
8. Cut margarine into small pieces with table knife and distribute over top.
9. Bake 30 to 35 minutes *or* until center springs back when pressed with mitt-covered finger. Serve warm.

CHOCOLATE PEANUT BUTTER PIE   C

MAKES: 6 to 8 servings

PREPARATION TIME: 30 minutes plus time to freeze

INGREDIENTS:
- ¼ cup chunky peanut butter
- ½ cup chocolate syrup
- 2 cups crisp rice cereal
- 1 quart French vanilla ice cream, softened
- ¼ cup chunky peanut butter
  Chocolate syrup
  Chopped peanuts

EQUIPMENT:
- 2 mixing spoons
- 2 mixing bowls
- 9-inch pie pan

1. Stir ¼ cup peanut butter and chocolate syrup with mixing spoon in mixing bowl.
2. Stir in cereal.
3. Spoon into pan. Press onto bottom and up sides of pan to form crust.

4. Stir ice cream and ¼ cup peanut butter with mixing spoon in another mixing bowl.

5. Spoon into crust.

6. Freeze until firm.

7. Remove pie from freezer 15 minutes before serving.

8. Drizzle with chocolate syrup and sprinkle with chopped peanuts. Serve immediately. Store leftovers in freezer.

MONSTER COOKIES   B

MAKES: 24

PREPARATION TIME: 20 minutes; 36 minutes to bake 3 sheets of cookies

INGREDIENTS:

2 eggs
½ cup butter *or* margarine, softened
½ cup light brown sugar, packed
½ cup granulated sugar
½ cup peanut butter
1 teaspoon vanilla
1½ cups flour
½ cup quick-cooking rolled oats
1 teaspoon baking soda
1 7-ounce bag candy-coated chocolate pieces (M & Ms) *or* 1 6-ounce package semisweet chocolate chips

EQUIPMENT:

mixing spoon
mixing bowl
baking sheet
metal spatula
wire rack

1. Preheat oven to 350°.

2. Stir eggs, butter, brown sugar, granulated sugar, peanut butter and vanilla with mixing spoon in mixing bowl.

3. Mix in remaining ingredients.

4. Drop 2 tablespoons dough for each cookie 3 inches apart on baking sheet.

5. Bake 10 to 12 minutes.

6. Remove cookies from baking sheet using spatula. Cool on rack. Store in airtight tin.

LAINA'S LOLLIPOP COOKIE TREATS   A

MAKES: about 18 cookies

PREPARATION TIME: 20 minutes; 15 minutes to bake

INGREDIENTS:

1 16-ounce roll refrigerator sugar cookie dough
2 2-ounce milk chocolate candy bars
18 popsicle sticks
   Chocolate frosting, if desired

EQUIPMENT:

sharp knife
baking sheets
wire rack
table knife

1. Preheat oven to 350°.

2. Slice cookie dough with knife into 36 slices and place half on baking sheets.

3. Break candy bars into individual squares.

4. Place a popsicle stick at the center of each cookie on half of the cookies.

5. Place a piece of chocolate on the tip of each popsicle stick.

6. Cover each chocolate piece with remaining cookies and slightly press edges together to enclose chocolate.

7. Place in oven; bake for about 12-15 minutes or until light brown.

8. Remove from oven; place on wire rack to cool.

9. When cool, spread a swirl of frosting with a table knife on each lollipop cookie, if desired.

THANKSGIVING HARVEST

Families gather for this long-celebrated American holiday to share turkey, cranberries and pumpkin prepared much the same way as the first Americans did in 1621. You can help make this great feast *or* use the delicious leftovers for the next day's dinner.

MAPLE-CINNAMON GRANOLA B

MAKES: 5 cups
PREPARATION TIME: 15 minutes; 1 hour
   to bake

INGREDIENTS:
  2 cups old-fashioned oatmeal
  ½ cup graham cracker crumbs
  ½ cup sesame seeds
  ½ cup chopped nuts
  ½ cup coconut
  ½ cup sunflower seeds
  ½ cup maple-flavored syrup
  ¼ cup vegetable oil
  ½ teaspoon cinnamon

EQUIPMENT:
   dry measuring cups
   liquid measuring cup
 1 large mixing bowl
   mixing spoon
   large shallow baking pan

1. Preheat oven to 250°.
2. Measure all ingredients into mixing bowl. Mix until all seeds and grains are coated with syrup and oil.
3. Pour granola into baking pan.
4. Place in oven; bake for 1 hour. Stir granola once or twice during the hour.
5. Remove from oven and cool.
6. Eat as breakfast cereal *or* as a snack.

HEARTY HARVEST SOUP A

MAKES: 6 servings
PREPARATION TIME: 25 minutes; 30 minutes to cook

INGREDIENTS:
 1 8-ounce can sliced carrots, drained
 1 16-ounce can tomatoes
 2 tablespoons instant minced onion
 2 cups water
 1 small zucchini *or* 1 8-ounce can
   green beans, drained
 2 cups cooked cubed ham
 1 cup uncooked macaroni
 1 teaspoon dried basil
 ½ teaspoon dried thyme
 ¼ teaspoon garlic powder
   Grated Parmesan cheese, optional

EQUIPMENT:
   4-quart soup kettle *or* saucepan
   with lid
   table knife

1. Combine carrots, tomatoes, onion and water in soup kettle.
2. Bring to boil over high heat.
3. Cut zucchini into small pieces using table knife.
4. Add zucchini, ham, macaroni, basil, thyme and garlic powder.
5. Turn heat to low.
6. Cover kettle. Simmer 30 minutes. Ladle soup into bowls.
7. Sprinkle with cheese, if desired.

Peanut Brittle Parfaits, page 41

THANKSGIVING HARVEST

HASH BROWN TURKEY   A

MAKES: 6 servings

PREPARATION TIME: 20 minutes; 40 minutes to bake

INGREDIENTS:

- 2 tablespoons butter *or* margarine
- 3 cups frozen hash brown potatoes
- 1 3-ounce can French-fried onions
- 6 to 8 thick slices cooked turkey
- 1 10-ounce can cream of chicken soup
- ½ cup dairy sour cream
- ¼ cup milk

EQUIPMENT:

     2-quart shallow baking pan *or* casserole
     mixing spoon
     small mixing bowl

1. Preheat oven to 425°.

2. Spread butter on bottom of pan.

3. Spread potatoes evenly over pan.

4. Bake 20 minutes *or* until potatoes start to brown.

5. Remove from oven. Reduce temperature to 375°.

6. Sprinkle onions over potatoes, reserving some for top.

7. Lay turkey slices on top of onions.

8. Stir soup, sour cream and milk with mixing spoon in mixing bowl. Pour over turkey.

9. Sprinkle with remaining onions.

10. Bake 20 minutes *or* until bubbling. Serve immediately.

CONFETTI CORN STUFFING BALLS   B

MAKES: 10 servings

PREPARATION TIME: 20 minutes; 15 minutes to bake

INGREDIENTS:

- 4 tablespoons butter, softened
- 3 cups seasoned stuffing mix
- 1 12-ounce can Mexican-style corn, drained
- 2 eggs
- ½ cup milk
- 1 tablespoon instant minced onion
- 4 tablespoons butter, softened

EQUIPMENT:

- 1 12-cup cupcake tin
     table knife
     mixing bowl
     mixing spoon
     ice cream scoop

1. Preheat oven to 375°. Grease tin.

2. Cut butter in small pieces with table knife. Put in mixing bowl.

3. Add remaining ingredients and stir with mixing spoon to combine. Let set 5 minutes.

4. Scoop mixture into tins using ice cream scoop.

5. Bake 15 minutes. Serve immediately.

PUMPKIN PATCH TORTES   C

MAKES: 12 servings

PREPARATION TIME: 20 minutes plus freezing time

INGREDIENTS:

- 1 quart butter pecan ice cream, softened
- ¾ cup canned pureed pumpkin
- ¼ cup light brown sugar, packed
- 1 teaspoon ground cinnamon
- 12 vanilla wafers
     Whipped cream, optional

EQUIPMENT:

     mixing spoon
     mixing bowl
- 12 paper cupcake liners
- 1 12-cup cupcake tin

1. Stir ice cream, pumpkin, brown sugar and cinnamon with mixing spoon in mixing bowl.

2. Put liners in muffin tin. Put 1 wafer in bottom of each liner.

3. Divide ice cream mixture equally among 12 liners.

4. Freeze several hours.

5. Remove liners and place tortes on small plates. Garnish each with spoonful of whipped cream, if desired. Serve immediately.

PEANUT BRITTLE PARFAITS   C

MAKES: 4 servings
PREPARATION TIME: 20 minutes
INGREDIENTS:

  1 3¾-ounce package instant
     butterscotch pudding mix
  ½ pound peanut brittle
     Whipped cream or topping

EQUIPMENT:

  mixing bowl
  rotary beater
  plastic bag
  rolling pin

1. Make pudding, according to package directions, in mixing bowl using rotary beater.

2. Put peanut brittle in plastic bag.

3. Gently hit with rolling pin to crush brittle.

4. Alternate layers of pudding and crushed peanut brittle in each of 4 dishes.

5. Sprinkle some crushed peanut brittle on top of each.

6. Top with dollop of whipped cream or topping. Serve immediately or refrigerate until serving time.

HARVEST APPLE CAKE   B

MAKES: 12 servings
PREPARATION TIME: 20 minutes; 50 minutes to bake

INGREDIENTS:

  1 17½-ounce package yellow cake
     mix
  3 eggs
  1 1-pound, 4-ounce can sliced apples
     for pie
  ½ cup dairy sour cream
  ¾ cup light brown sugar, packed
  2 tablespoons flour
  1 teaspoon ground cinnamon
  2 tablespoons butter or margarine,
     softened

EQUIPMENT:

  1 10-inch Bundt pan
     mixing spoon
  1 large mixing bowl
  1 small mixing bowl
     wire rack
     table knife

1. Preheat oven to 350°. Generously grease pan.

2. Stir cake mix, eggs, apples and sour cream with mixing spoon in large mixing bowl until batter is smooth.

3. Stir brown sugar, flour, cinnamon and butter with mixing spoon in small mixing bowl.

4. Pour ½ batter into pan.

5. Sprinkle with ½ crumb mixture.

6. Top with remaining batter and remaining crumbs.

7. Bake 40 to 50 minutes.

8. Cool on rack 15 minutes.

9. Loosen edges of cake from pan with table knife.

10. Remove cake from pan. Cool completely.

Christmas is a time for great rejoicing and good will. The air is filled with anticipation at the arrival of, none other than, Santa Claus. Your help in preparing a few meals during this busy time would be a welcome gift to your parents. Share these holiday foods with family and friends!

HOLIDAY PUNCH WITH FRUIT RING   C

MAKES: 8 servings
PREPARATION TIME: 20 minutes plus freezing time

INGREDIENTS:
- 4 cups water
- 12 maraschino cherries
- 1 6-ounce can frozen orange juice concentrate, thawed
- 2 cups cranberry juice, chilled
- 1 quart lemon-lime soda, chilled

EQUIPMENT:
- 5-cup ring mold
- 3-quart punch bowl
- mixing spoon
- dish towel

1. Make ice ring, 1 day before serving, by pouring 1 cup water in mold. Evenly space cherries on bottom of mold. Freeze. When firm, add remaining 3 cups water. Freeze.

2. Next day, pour concentrate and cranberry juice into punch bowl. Stir with mixing spoon until blended.

3. Soak towel in hot water; squeeze to remove most of water. Place on bottom of mold to loosen ice ring. Place ring in punch bowl.

4. Stir in soda. Serve immediately.

CRISPY CHRISTMAS WREATH   A

MAKES: 8 to 10 servings
PREPARATION TIME: 25 minutes

INGREDIENTS:
- 1 ¾-ounce package Italian dressing mix
- ½ cup mayonnaise
- ½ cup dairy sour cream
- 1 tablespoon vegetable oil
- 2 tablespoons vinegar
- ½ teaspoon ground dried thyme
- 1 green pepper
- 2 cups raw cauliflower pieces
- 2 cups raw broccoli pieces
- 1 pint cherry tomatoes

EQUIPMENT:
- mixing spoon
- small mixing bowl
- sharp knife
- round platter
- small serving bowl

1. Stir all ingredients except vegetables with mixing spoon in mixing bowl.

2. Chill.

3. Wash all vegetables.

4. Cut green pepper into thin strips using sharp knife.

5. Place vegetable pieces around rim of platter.

6. Pour dip in serving bowl and put in middle of vegetables. Serve immediately.

Crispy Christmas Wreath, Holiday Punch with Fruit Ring, this page; Banana Nog, page 44

CHRISTMAS

BANANA NOG   A

MAKES: 4 servings
PREPARATION TIME: 10 minutes

INGREDIENTS:
  1 ripe banana
  1 egg
  2 tablespoons granulated sugar or honey
  3 cups milk
  2 scoops vanilla ice cream
    Pinch grated nutmeg
EQUIPMENT:
    blender

1. Peel banana, break into pieces and place in container of blender with remaining ingredients.

2. Blend on medium-high speed until smooth and frosty.

3. Pour into 4 glasses.

COMPANY'S COMING HAM   B

MAKES: 4 to 6 servings
PREPARATION TIME: 10 minutes; 20 minutes to bake

INGREDIENTS:
  1 pound boneless, cooked ham slices, ¼-inch thick
  ½ cup sour cherry preserves or jam or whole-berry cranberry sauce
  2 tablespoons vinegar
  ½ teaspoon ground cloves
  ½ teaspoon dry mustard
EQUIPMENT:
    8 × 10-inch baking dish
    mixing spoon
    mixing bowl

1. Preheat oven to 350°. Grease dish.

2. Arrange ham slices in dish.

3. Stir remaining ingredients with mixing spoon in mixing bowl.

4. Spread over ham.

5. Bake 15 to 20 minutes until ham is heated through and preserves bubble. Serve immediately.

SNOW-CAPPED GREEN BEANS   B

MAKES: 4 servings
PREPARATION TIME: 10 minutes; 20 minutes to bake

INGREDIENTS:
  1 tablespoon butter or margarine
  1 3-ounce can sliced mushrooms
  1 9-ounce package frozen French-style green beans, thawed
  ½ teaspoon salt
  ½ teaspoon dried basil
  1 cup dairy sour cream
EQUIPMENT:
    1-quart casserole
    spoon
    aluminum foil

1. Preheat oven to 350°.

2. Spread butter on bottom of casserole.

3. Top with mushrooms.

4. Spread green beans over mushrooms.

5. Sprinkle with salt and basil.

6. Spoon sour cream over top.

7. Cover loosely with foil.

8. Bake 20 minutes or until mixture starts to bubble around edges. Serve immediately.

MERRY SANTAS   C

MAKES: 5 servings
PREPARATION TIME: 20 minutes

INGREDIENTS:
   1 quart strawberry ice cream
  12 semisweet chocolate chips
   6 maraschino cherries
   6 sugar cones
   1 cup grated coconut
   1 7-ounce aerosol can whipped cream
EQUIPMENT:
    6 dessert plates
      ice cream scoop

1. Place large scoop of ice cream in center of each plate using ice cream scoop.

2. Place 2 chocolate chips on ice cream for eyes.

3. Add 1 maraschino cherry for nose.

4. Break off tip of cone and place on plate at top of ice cream scoop.

5. Sprinkle 2 to 3 tablespoons coconut around ice cream scoop to resemble "fur collar."

6. Place whipped cream on ice cream to resemble beard and around edge of cone and at cone tip to make "fur trim." Repeat with remaining 5 desserts.

7. Freeze or serve immediately.

GRANDMA'S BROWNIE-MINT COOKIES   B

MAKES: 30

PREPARATION TIME: 20 minutes; 30 minutes to bake 3 sheets of cookies

INGREDIENTS:
- 1 cup granulated sugar
- ½ cup butter or margarine, softened
- 2 eggs
- 2 1-ounce packages unsweetened liquid chocolate flavoring or 2 1-ounce squares unsweetened chocolate, melted
- 1 teaspoon baking powder
- 1 cup flour
- ¼ teaspoon salt
- 1 teaspoon vanilla
- ½ cup chopped nuts
- ½ cup crushed peppermint candies

EQUIPMENT:
- baking sheet
- mixing spoon
- mixing bowl
- teaspoon
- metal spatula
- wire rack

1. Preheat oven to 350°. Grease baking sheet.

2. Stir sugar, butter and eggs with mixing spoon in mixing bowl.

3. Stir in chocolate.

4. Blend in all remaining ingredients.

5. Drop dough by teaspoon 2 inches apart on baking sheet.

6. Bake 8 to 9 minutes. Don't overbake.

7. Place cookies on rack using spatula to cool completely. Store in airtight tin.

CARAMEL-PECAN CRUNCHIES   A

MAKES: 64

PREPARATION TIME: 25 minutes

INGREDIENTS:
- 20 marshmallows
- 20 vanilla caramel candies
- 2 tablespoons water
- 2 tablespoons butter
- 1 teaspoon vanilla
- 3 cups crisp rice cereal
- ½ cup chopped pecans

EQUIPMENT:
- 9-inch square baking pan
- wooden spoon
- 3-quart saucepan

1. Grease pan.

2. Stir marshmallows, caramels, water and butter with wooden spoon in saucepan over low heat until caramels and marshmallows melt.

3. Remove from heat. Stir in vanilla.

4. Stir in cereal and nuts until well coated with caramel mixture.

5. Press into baking pan using mixing spoon.

6. Cool.

7. Cut into 1-inch squares using table knife dipped in hot water. Store in airtight tin.